PREHISTORIC WORLD

EARLY LIFE

Dougal Dixon

ticktock

Copyright © 2006 *ticktock* Entertainment Ltd. First published in Great Britain by ticktock Media Ltd.,
Unit 2, Orchard Business Centre, North Farm Road, Tunbridge Wells, Kent TN2 3XF, Great Britain.

A CIP catalogue record for this book is available from the British Library.

ISBN 1 84696 032 0

Printed in China

CONTENTS

INTRODUCTION

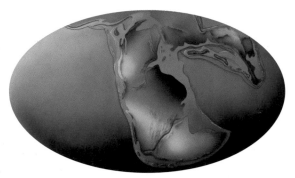

This map shows how the Earth looked at the end of the Palaeozoic Era. Most of the Earth's continents are grouped into one mass of land.

This map shows how the Earth looks today. See how different it is! The continents have split up and moved around.

Prehistoric World is a series of six books that follows the evolution of animals.

The Earth's history is divided into sections called eras, which are then divided into periods. These last millions of years. Each book in this series looks at the most exciting animals from prehistory periods.

This book is about the Palaeozoic Era. At the beginning of it animals with bony parts developed. These parts became fossilised. Our knowledge of this era comes from these fossils. In this time the first land animals also evolved.

PREHISTORIC WORLD TIMELINE

Use this timeline to trace prehistoric life. It shows how simple creatures evolved into more different kinds.
This took millions and millions of years. That is what MYA stands for – millions of years ago.

		BOOK	PERIOD	
CENOZOIC ERA		THE ICE AGE	1.75 MYA to now QUATERNARY	*This is a period of ice ages and mammals. Our direct relatives, Homo sapiens, also appear.*
		ANCIENT MAMMALS	65 to 1.75 MYA TERTIARY	*Giant mammals and huge, hunting birds appear in this period. Our first human relatives also start to evolve.*
MESOZOIC ERA		CRETACEOUS LIFE	135 to 65 MYA CRETACEOUS	*Huge dinosaurs evolve. They all die by the end of this period.*
		JURASSIC LIFE	203 to 135 MYA JURASSIC	*Large and small dinosaurs and flying creatures develop.*
		TRIASSIC LIFE	250 to 203 MYA TRIASSIC	*The 'Age of Dinosaurs' begins. Mammals also start to appear.*
PALAEOZOIC ERA		EARLY LIFE	295 to 250 MYA PERMIAN	*Sail-backed reptiles start to appear.*
			355 to 295 MYA CARBONIFEROUS	*The first reptiles appear and tropical forests develop.*
			410 to 355 MYA DEVONIAN	*Bony fish evolve. Trees and insects appear.*
			435 to 410 MYA SILURIAN	*Fish with jaws develop and land creatures appear.*
			500 to 435 MYA ORDOVICIAN	*Primitive fishes, trilobites, shellfish and plants evolve.*
			540 to 500 MYA CAMBRIAN	*First animals with skeletons appear.*

PARADOXIDES

Paradoxides belonged to a group of animals called the trilobites. These were the most important sea-living animals of the Cambrian Period. There were no land-living animals at this time. Trilobites were covered in a shell made of material similar to your nails. They also had jointed legs. Shrimps have similar shells.

There were thousands of different kinds of trilobites. They all had a big head shield and a tail shield, and the body in between consisted of moveable segments. Some trilobites could swim, some could burrow, and others could roll up into a ball.

ANIMAL
FACTFILE

NAME: *Paradoxides* (like a puzzle)

PRONOUNCED: par-oh-dox-ee-dees

GROUP: Trilobite

WHERE IT LIVED: Canada, Europe, North Africa

WHEN IT LIVED: Early to middle Cambrian Period (570 to 517 million years ago)

LENGTH: 25 cm

SPECIAL FEATURES: Spines at the edge of each body segment

FOOD: Particles on the seabed

MAIN ENEMY: Big arthropods

DID YOU KNOW?: *Paradoxides* was one of the first trilobites to evolve.

Paradoxides (on the right of this picture) was one of the biggest trilobites. It was hunted by even bigger animals, like the fearsome *Anomalocaris* that you see here.

ORTHOCERAS

In the early part of the Palaeozoic Era, all animals lived in the sea. *Orthoceras* was the biggest hunter of the time, and could grow up to 1 metre long. It looked like an octopus, in a long straight shell. *Orthoceras* caught other animals with its strong tentacles.

With its streamlined shell *Orthoceras* could chase after its prey. By squirting water it could push itself forwards in very quick bursts.

ANIMAL
FACTFILE

NAME: *Orthoceras* (straight shell)

PRONOUNCED: orth-oh-seer-us

GROUP: Cephalopod

WHERE IT LIVED: Worldwide

WHEN IT LIVED: Ordovician Period (510 to 439 million years ago)

LENGTH: From 15 cm to 1 metre

SPECIAL FEATURES: Shell with many chambers in it

FOOD: Other sea animals

MAIN ENEMY: None

DID YOU KNOW?: *Orthoceras* fossils are relatively common. We often see the polished shells of *Orthoceras* in fossil shops.

The shell of *Orthoceras* had many chambers. With the chambers full of air *Orthoceras* could float. To sink down it would have filled the chambers with water.

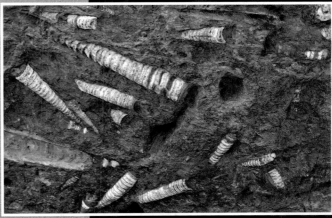

DIPLOGRAPTUS

In the surface waters of early Palaeozoic times lived tiny creatures that looked like jellyfish. They were called graptolites. The *Diplograptus* you see here were a type of graptolite. They had two rows of cups back to back. Each cup contained an animal. The cups were attached to a UFO-shaped unit. This is called a float. Graptolite colonies floated through the oceans anchored to their floats.

A graptolite colony looked like the blade of a saw. Each 'tooth' was a tiny cup that held an individual animal. Colonies consisted of dozens of these individuals attached together.

NAME: *Diplograptus* (double graptolite)

PRONOUNCED: dip-low-grap-tus

GROUP: Graptolite

WHERE IT LIVED: Worldwide, in all the oceans

WHEN IT LIVED: Late Ordovician Period (443 to 439 million years ago)

LENGTH: each string was about 10 cm

SPECIAL FEATURES: Two rows of cups back to back

FOOD: Floating organic matter

MAIN ENEMY: None

DID YOU KNOW?: Other graptolite colonies have names based on how the cups were arranged. *Monograptus* had a single row of cups, *Tetragraptus* had four rows of cups, *Didymograptus* had two separate rows

Each tiny graptolite organism in the colony had a feathery feeding organ that trailed in the water. These gathered floating food particles.

CEPHALASPIS

Fish evolved at the beginning of the Palaeozoic Era. The first fish, like *Cephalaspis*, had no jaws, just a sucker for a mouth. *Cephalaspis* did not have much of a skeleton either – just a backbone and a skull. Its head was protected by an armoured shield, like that of a trilobite.

Cephalaspis fed from the bottom of streams and lakes. The fin on the underside of its tail kept the head downwards, and the sucker mouth could sift for food in the sand of the bed.

ANIMAL FACTFILE

NAME: *Cephalaspis* (head-shield fish)

PRONOUNCED: sef-al-as-pis

GROUP: Agnatha – the jawless fish

WHERE IT LIVED: Freshwater in Northern Europe

WHEN IT LIVED: Devonian Period (408 to 362 million years ago)

LENGTH: 12 cm

SPECIAL FEATURES: *Cephalaspis* may have had electric organs on its head. They would have given an electric shock to any predator that tried to attack.

FOOD: Organic scraps on the river bed

MAIN ENEMY: Big arthropods like giant scorpions

DID YOU KNOW?: It was from little fish like this that the whole range of modern backboned animals evolved.

These fossil fish were the earliest of the vertebrates – the animals with backbones.

DUNKLEOSTEUS

The Devonian Period of the Palaeozoic Era was called the 'Age of Fish'. There were many different kinds of fish that lived in the deep oceans, the shallow seas and in the rivers. Little fish lived on small scraps of food, but some of the big fish were the fierce hunters of the time. *Dunkleosteus* was one of the biggest and fiercest.

Dunkleosteus belonged to a group of fish that had armoured heads and necks. The smooth shape of the bony head armour gave the fish a teardrop shape. This helped it speed through the water as it hunted smaller fish to eat.

ANIMAL
FACTFILE

NAME: *Dunkleosteus* (Dunkle's bony one, after the person who discovered it)

PRONOUNCED: dunk-el-ost-ee-us

GROUP: Arthrodire – the jointed necked fish

WHERE IT LIVED: North America

WHEN IT LIVED: Late Devonian Period (370 to 360 million years ago)

LENGTH: 9 metres

SPECIAL FEATURES: Scissor-like blades on the powerful jaws

FOOD: Other fish

MAIN ENEMY: None

DID YOU KNOW?: The head and neck are most often found as fossils, because they were so heavily armoured.

This frightening creature must have been the terror of the late Palaeozoic seas. Instead of teeth it had sharp blades, like carving knives, on the sides of its jaws. These were curved into hooks at the front for seizing prey.

TIKTAALIK

Among the fish of the Devonian Period, there
were a few that could spend some time out of
the water. These had lungs and were able to
breathe air. They would not have been able
to spend much time on land, but they were
the first backboned animals to do so.
Tiktaalik was one of these.

Tiktaalik had bony fins. These had a shoulder, elbow and wrist. This means the fins worked a bit like legs. The skull was more like a crocodile's, than a fish.

Tiktaalik lived in streams and ponds. When these dried up in hot weather, it was able to use its ability to crawl over land to find new ponds in which to live.

ANIMAL FACTFILE

NAME: *Tiktaalik* (a native word for a big fish)

PRONOUNCED: tik-ta-lick

GROUP: Crossopterygian — with fins that could move them on land or in the water

WHERE IT LIVED: Northern Canada

WHEN IT LIVED: Late Devonian Period (375 million years ago)

LENGTH: 2.7 metres

SPECIAL FEATURES: Two pairs of fins that acted like legs, lungs that allowed it to breathe on land

FOOD: Small fish or arthropods

MAIN ENEMY: Bigger fish

DID YOU KNOW?: There are fish today, such as the mudskipper of the tropics, that can spend time on land.

CHTHYOSTEGA

Ichthyostega is the earliest amphibian that we know about. Although it had the body, legs and toes of a land-living animal, it had the head of a fish and a fishy fin on the tail. This shows that its ancestors were fish.

Ichthyostega probably had a lifestyle quite similar to the mudskipper, found in tropical regions today. Mudskippers are fish, but they have special adaptations that allow them to spend time on land.

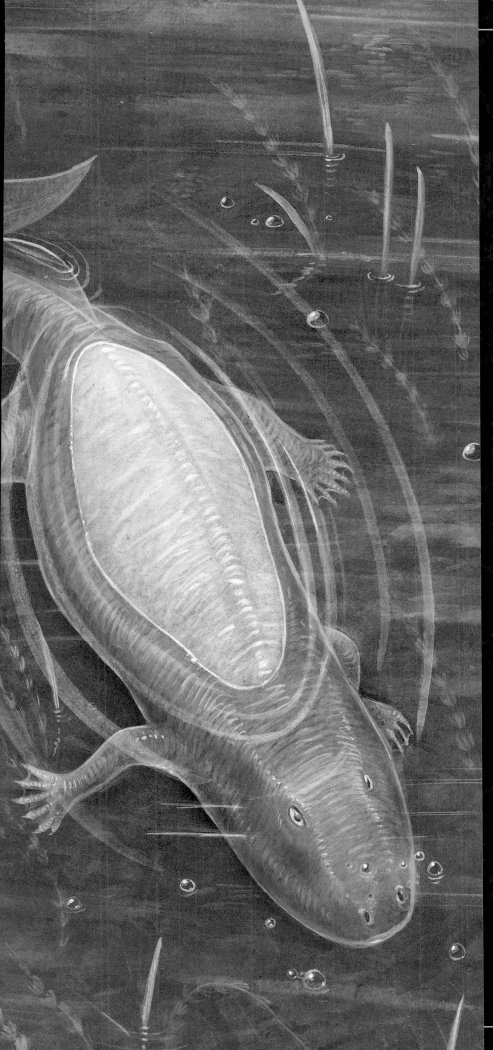

ANIMAL
FACTFILE

NAME: *Ichthyostega* (fish skull)

PRONOUNCED: ick-thee-oh-stay-ga

GROUP: Labyrinthodon — the earliest amphibians

WHERE IT LIVED: Greenland

WHEN IT LIVED: Late Devonian Period (377 – 362 million years ago)

LENGTH: 1 metre

SPECIAL FEATURES: Strong shoulders and hips, to work the legs and feet

FOOD: Insects and other small animals

MAIN ENEMY: Big fish

DID YOU KNOW?: A strange thing about *Ichthyostega* is the number of its toes. It had eight toes on the hind foot and six on the front. Later backboned animals would have a maximum of five toes on each foot.

Even though it was adapted to living on land, *Ichthyostega* probably spent most of its time in the water. Its feet helped it push its way through thick water weeds.

CRASSIGYRINUS

By the time of the Carboniferous Period, many amphibians were able to spend more time on land. However, some amphibians adapted to spend their lives completely in the water. *Crassigyrinus* was one of these.

Crassigyrinus was like a big eel (as above), swimming along with powerful swings of its huge tail. Its tiny front limbs acted as balancing fins.

ANIMAL
FACTFILE

NAME: *Crassigyrinus* (thick frog)

PRONOUNCED: crass-ig-ee-ri-nus

GROUP: Embolomere – one of the amphibian groups

WHERE IT LIVED: Scotland

WHEN IT LIVED: Early Carboniferous Period (349 to 332 million years ago)

LENGTH: 2 metres

SPECIAL FEATURES: The skull was heavy and the jaws strong – together they would have produced a bone-crushing fish trap

FOOD: Other amphibians and fish

MAIN ENEMY: Even bigger amphibians and fish

DID YOU KNOW?: *Crassigyrinus* had a mouth with sharp needle-like teeth and jaws that snapped shut like a trap.

Crassigyrinus had big eyes. They would have helped it to find its way through the dark, murky, weed-choked waters of the Carboniferous swamps.

WESTLOTHIANA

The big difference between amphibians and reptiles is the fact that reptiles can lay their eggs on land. While amphibians need to lay their eggs in water, *Westlothiana* was probably able to lay its eggs on land. This would make it the first reptile.

Westlothiana looked just like a little lizard. It probably lived like one too, chasing insects through the undergrowth.

Only one fossil of *Westlothiana* has been found,

and that was in a quarry where there were also fossils of spiders, scorpions and land plants. They all lived together in swampy forest.

ANIMAL FACTFILE

NAME: *Westlothiana* (from West Lothian, the county in Scotland where it was found)

PRONOUNCED: west-low-thee-ah-na

GROUP: Possibly a very early reptile

WHERE IT LIVED: Scotland

WHEN IT LIVED: Early Carboniferous Period (338 million years ago)

LENGTH: 30 cm

SPECIAL FEATURES: Ability to lay eggs and live on land full time

FOOD: Insects and spiders

MAIN ENEMY: *Brontoscorpio*, a giant scorpion about 1 metre long

DID YOU KNOW?: Although we think *Westlothiana* was a reptile, its skeleton is very similar to that of an amphibian. *Westlothiana* shows how reptiles developed from amphibians.

DIMETRODON

The Permian Period was the last period of the Palaeozoic Era. When it began, deserts covered most of Earth. *Dimetrodon* was a reptile that was well adapted to living in the hot, dry conditions.

In the cold desert mornings *Dimetrodon* could hold up the sail on its back to the Sun, to warm itself. In the heat of the day, wind passing over the sail would cool it down.

Dimetrodon had two types of teeth. This is unusual for a reptile. It had long teeth in front to cut through meat, and short ones behind to tear it into small pieces.

ANIMAL FACTFILE

NAME: *Dimetrodon* (two kinds of teeth)

PRONOUNCED: di-met-ro-don

GROUP: Pelycosaur

WHERE IT LIVED: Texas

WHEN IT LIVED: Early Permian Period (290 to 256 million years ago)

LENGTH: 3.3 metres

SPECIAL FEATURES: Tall spines covered by skin, forming a sail on its back

FOOD: Other reptiles

MAIN ENEMY: None

DID YOU KNOW?: Many people wrongly think that *Dimetrodon* was a dinosaur. It lived a long time before the dinosaurs and was not related at all.

LYCAENOPS

Lycaenops had a long skull with sharp teeth and long legs for running fast. It may have lived in packs. Many scientists think it looked and behaved rather like a wolf. Permian reptiles like *Lycaenops* were the distant ancestors of the mammals.

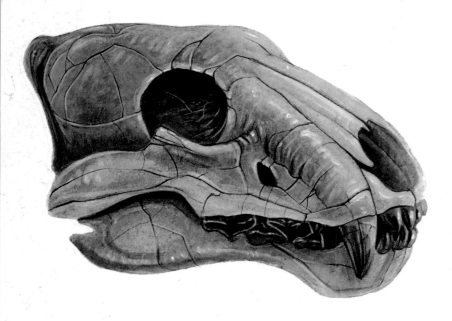

Lycaenops had killing teeth at the front of its mouth, and meat-shredding teeth at the back. Modern wolves use their teeth in the same way.

ANIMAL
FACTFILE

NAME: *Lycaenops* (looking like
a dog)

PRONOUNCED: lie-kee-nops

GROUP: Gorgonopsian – one of the
groups of mammal-like reptiles

WHERE IT LIVED: South Africa

WHEN IT LIVED: Late Permian Period
(256 to 245 million years ago)

LENGTH: 1 metre

SPECIAL FEATURES: Dog-like
or wolf-like teeth

FOOD: Other reptiles

MAIN ENEMY: Bigger meat-eating
reptiles

DID YOU KNOW?: *Lycaenops* had
legs close to its body (like mammals
today) not out to the side (like a
crocodile's legs). This helped it to
run faster than the other animals
of the time.

There were bigger hunting
reptiles around at the time,
but *Lycaenops* would have
been a fierce predator
of smaller reptiles.

ESTEMMENOSUCHUS

In the Permian Period, a lot of the land was desert. Not all parts of the desert were dry and lifeless. Some areas had small lakes or streams where plants could grow. These areas were inhabited by big plant-eating reptiles. *Estemmenosuchus* was about the size of a hippopotamus!

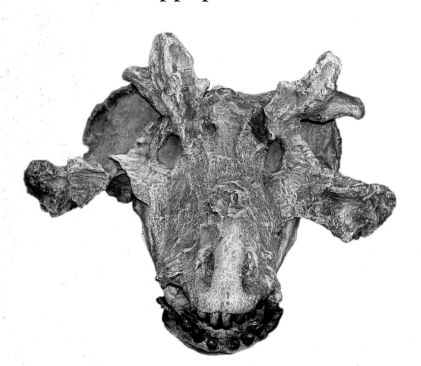

The strange thing about *Estemmenosuchus* was the bumps and horns on the head. They may have been used to tell each other apart, or they may have been used as weapons. Perhaps they head-butted one another like bulls.

ANIMAL FACTFILE

NAME: *Estemmenosuchus* (crowned crocodile)

PRONOUNCED: es-tem-en-oh-sook-us

GROUP: Dinocephalia – a group of the mammal-like reptiles

WHERE IT LIVED: Eastern Russia

WHEN IT LIVED: The late Permian Period (256 to 245 million years ago)

LENGTH: 4 metres

SPECIAL FEATURES: Horns around the head

FOOD: Plants

MAIN ENEMY: Gorgonopsians such as *Lycaenops* and its relatives

DID YOU KNOW?: Even though *Estemmenosuchus* looked so fierce and had big teeth, the teeth were only adapted for eating plants.

Estemmenosuchus probably lived in small herds, munching away at the fern-like plants and conifers that formed the main vegetation at the time.

ANIMAL FAMILIES GLOSSARY

Agnatha — the most primitive fish type. They lacked jaws and had a sucker for a mouth, like the modern lamprey, and lived mostly in Silurian and Devonian times.

Arthrodire — a primitive group of fish with armoured heads and necks. The name means "jointed neck" and refers to the arrangement of armour. They were the terror of Devonian seas.

Arthropod — the invertebrates with the outside shell and jointed legs. They include the modern insects, crabs and spiders. The shell is made of material like your fingernails.

Cephalopod — literally the "head-footed" animals. The modern types, the octopus and squid, seem to have legs branching from their faces. In prehistoric times many of them had chambered shells.

Crossopterygian — the fish that could spend some time on land. They had lungs and muscular fins, and gave rise to the amphibians.

Dicynodont — the group of mammal-like reptiles that had a pair of teeth at the front that looked like those of a dog. They were mostly plant-eaters.

Embolomere — a group of Carboniferous amphibians with very long bodies that swam in fresh water by twisting like eels.

Gorgonopsian — a fierce group of mammal-like reptiles, looking like a cross between a crocodile and a sabre-toothed tiger, living mainly in Permian and early Triassic times.

Graptolite — a group of tiny sea-living animals that consisted of a string of individuals attached to a stalk. They floated in the waters of the Ordovician and Silurian seas.

Labyrinthodon — one of the groups of early amphibians, from the Carboniferous and Permian Periods. They were so-called because the enamel of the teeth was contorted like a labyrinth, or maze.

Pelycosaur — the most primitive group of the mammal-like reptiles, from early Permian times. Most of them had big fins on their backs. Some were meat-eaters and others were plant-eaters.

Trilobite — a group of common sea-living arthropods, common from Cambrian to Devonian times, that had head shields, tail shields, and the body divided into segments in between.

GLOSSARY

Adapted — changing to survive in a particular habitat or weather conditions.

Amphibian — an animal that is able to live on both land and water.

Ancestors — an early form of the animal group that lived in the past.

Cold-blooded — animals, such as reptiles or amphibians, which rely on their environment to control their body temperature.

Colonies — groups of animals of the same kind living closely together.

Conifer — an evergreen tree such as a pine or fir.

Continents — the world's main land masses such as Africa and Europe.

Dinosaur — large group of meat-eating or plant-eating reptiles that no longer exist.

Evolution — changes or developments that happen to all forms of life over millions of years, as a result of changes in the environment.

Evolve — to change or develop.

Fossils — the remains of a prehistoric plant or animal that has been buried for a long time and become hardened in rock.

Fossilised — to turn into a fossil.

Mammal — a warm-blooded animal which is covered in hair. The female gives birth to live young and produces milk from her own body to feed them.

Meat-shearing teeth — special teeth that are used to cut or slice the flesh from bones.

Organic matter — really tiny animal or plant life.

Palaeozoic Era — the period when life first appeared on Earth.

Predators — animals that hunt and kill other animals for food.

Prehistory — a time before humans evolved.

Prey — animals that are hunted by other animals as food.

Primitive — a very early stage in the development of a species.

Reptiles — cold-blooded, crawling or creeping animals with a backbone.

Segments — divided into separate parts.

Sift — to separate food from water when feeding.

Species — a group of animals which all look like each other.

Tropics — hot countries that are close to the equator.

INDEX

PICTURE CREDITS

Main illustrations: 8-9, 12-13, 24-25 Simon Mendez; 6-7, 20-21, 28-29 Luis Rey;
10-11, 14-15, 16-17, 18-19, 22-23, 26-27 Chris Tomlin

4 TL, 4TR, 5 (Cenozoic Era), 6, 9, 10, 13, 14, 17 Ticktock Media archive; 5 (Mesozoic Era top, Palaeozoic Era top),
23 Simon Mendez; 5 (Mesozoic Era centre, Palaeozoic Era bottom) Luis Rey; 5 (Mesozoic Era bottom) Lisa Alderson;
18 Hu Lan /Alamy; 20 Shutterstock; 25 Mervyn Rees/Alamy; 26 Chris Tomlin; 28 Gondwana Studios

Every effort has been made to trace the copyright holders and we apologise in advance for any unintentional omissions.
We would be pleased to insert the appropriate acknowledgement in any subsequent edition of this publication.